Whirligig

Christopher Salerno

SPUYTEN DUYVIL
New York City

Acknowledgements are hereby made to the editors of the following journals for the first publication of some of the poems in *Whirligig*, many of which appear in different versions:

Jubilat, Colorado Review, Free Verse, AGNI-online, Spinning Jenny, Forklift Ohio, LIT, GoodFoot, Carolina Quarterly, The Tiny, Main Street Rag, 5AM, Electronic Poetry Review, Barrow Street, Diner, River City, Tar River Poetry, Bennington Review, Beacon Street Review, Asheville Poetry Review, Can We Have Our Ball Back, Sunstone Magazine, Blood and Fire Review.

"Between The Lions" was reprinted in the anthology, "The Bedside Guide To No Tell Motel" (2005).

Many poems appearing here also appear in the chapbook, "Waving Something White," (University Book Exchange's Independent Press, 2003).

The author would like to express his gratitude and thanks to Ed Ochester, Liam Rector, April Bernard, Jason Shinder, Mary Carroll Hackett, Russell Dillon, Paul Mazza, Lacy Simons, Eliot Treichel, Chris Tonelli, Tom Lisk, my family, and Robin who gave me the time and support.

Library of Congress Cataloging-in-Publication Data

Salerno, Christopher, 1975-
Whirligig / Christopher Salerno.
p. cm.
Includes bibliographical references.
ISBN-13: 978-1-933132-26-6
I. Title.

PS3619.A435W47 2006
811'.6--dc22
2006004576

Printed in Canada

CONTENTS

III.

In memory of Christopher Gulick

Part One

A COUNTY

Little good, the profundity of flying over iris fields
when we land ululating. Wheel-sparks
jump to a thin riot's tune. *Not the usual blues*
I write in my daybook, with its rubbings
of a disproportionate world
whose constellations throb and that is what aches.
Around our heads, day is not yet dark.
It is still lovely to see: Waitresses
pedal in the direction of the city—
the muscles in their calves slowly waking
and curving to a point. Do you get the picture
of a place you have left entirely up to me?
Tire tracks in raked gravel. Walking-sticks in the distance.
A sign by the road reads: *This Is The County
You've Entered.* Each night, a sky all dressed up.
The moon, a white boutonniere.
Stars winking business of the past,
as if to say, in so many years
what will crack up and fall will have
threaded an atmosphere, since the need to reenter
is coupled with a tendency to burn.

BURYING A ST. JOSEPH IN THE BACKYARD

He has never been called loser; he is digging a hole.
The sun throws in its voice. Cirrus clouds
he must be mostly absent to see. If he prays
for a higher offer, the words are unknown to anyone
like a room that is empty and dark. There,
he watches his own shadow, with all its weight,
packing curtains in a hard-shell case.
Summer is going and taking with it every clear idea
the windows ever had, giving way
to an ever-expanding emptiness. Now, only X
marks the weedy spot where what is buried
slowly loses form. Nights: A net of mosquitoes
in a capital hangs dusklit on each light.
Dew uncurls the fists of dry leaves along the patio.
He holds. As now his dogs dig up
the textured clay and bring it in the house.
He clears a space nowhere in particular. For a moment,
there isn't a Weehawken. Around his head,
bubble wrap. He is breaking it and breathing in.

Through which the eye learns how to render
the entire valley. We also need a sample,
somehow, of the bad lighting
our mothers have been photographed in—
heels clicking in 4/4 time,
which alone has hurled them
back like those reverse Hendrix solos
from *Axis Bold As Love*
they were never meant for.

Another way of locating what's been lost
is through a long marooning
with a medal of St. Anthony
and an empty canvas—
to muse out corpuscles
of old subjects tirelessly
all the rest of our lives.
What we objectify to find again.
The last fact of it is
it will be dark in one hour.
The masculine backdrops of late day
crouch like fired men
on the border of a train yard
and the huge abyss.

ON THE LAKE WITH ERROR

Every day for a week
on this stretch of beach,
you have hidden
my one good oar, wobbled
each spiral I've thrown—
my Spring hypotheses
landing in the brush
like tinfoil swans.
There were days too
I had to lie down.
How was I to know
by *Unzip the lake!*
you meant *Full speed ahead!*
Avoid yacht-wake!
Did I think the deep
had something to release?
What I want to know
how to read the lake
in which we are framed.
How to sing
apostrophic ditties
in the underwater cathedral
of the Academy.
Who could go on trying?
Error, as you lift the body,
efforts elsewhere
go quiet. My wet pants
cling to skin.
When a phone rings,
I dance to it.

COLLECTED MARGINALIA

All are collected and checked for obscenity.

                                              Each one
a possible beginning:
The sentiments of lovers

                                              one note lower than
sound.

"If I painted you w/out genitalia, w/out identity,

with all white flowers
folded in—

                              above you your shadow,
                              a slow pulse, acquiring you—"

How else to paint the woman in the middle of the room?

For those who stand beneath
the painting there
is no repose.

                              Pointing out how your shadow
                              takes you

Missionary style.
Its ends no ends at all.

                              How it comes, now,
                    grasping
                              at your life, they'll say

before tossing their thick glasses into the fire.

SMOKE ON THE WATER

After the three-hour ride and the classic rock,
we arrive. The home swings its gate.

The yard-dogs piddle themselves from
the high-pitched screech of the hinge.

I must be triggering a silent alarm—
I mean the scarecrow sprouts hair, and only

in the back. From his jean jacket come
shards of jar glass, a photo slightly burned

around its edges. Who could be closer
to the truth? I nearly sing: *Synaptic garden hose,*

bring word, deliver me news. Live Oak, multiply,
and do not leave. Instead, I turn to just

one more dream, not yet remembering
how we lived forever in this bungalow,

strumming along on its porch. I wait
for the mailman—his Walkman up so loud

I can hear the faint, tinny symphony—
he delivers catalogues for a fire prone sky.

Seller says: "Home includes
sound of slight pounding.
In the spring, on days like
these, you can lie in the
woodshed thinking of old
dance partners—what they
must smell like now!" Seller
says: "Updated swivel,
updated downspouts.
Interior plan brings outside
in. Good transitional space.
O landscape! O field! Field
has potential mountain
inside."

WHIRLIGIG

The world's smallest:
Ass pushed out, head hammering air, repeating:

Yes to wind, yes to all night.

You remain, rider who is not a rider,
        a He.

Scripted hand all day

                                        reaching
                                        in a whir:
Up a cowboy boot.
On a warm border,
                for a bubble in the path of a bullet.

We're alone in our best visions.

        Right down to
        the calcified ground.
        Eyes on our middle
        hill. Eyes on hands, we slip
        into weather for its constant flux,
        its freedom to eat the air,
        which begins *and* ends
        with what is right now stirring—
        how every plot starts:
        We attach to desire
        the inching of a toy.

TONIGHT WE'RE GOING TO PARTY LIKE IT'S 1799

Not a tincture of water for the first.
If *the roof* is indeed *on fire*.
    Oh yeah, a moody sky, but not a rainy one.
    And if it's a solid mile to the pond?
        If the woods are full of strong owls?
        The story is men uncover
            the yard, they pack the house with dirt.
        They slide all furniture
            against the walls. Death and the beautifully
            painted door open at once.
                A few drift into it.
                It is in this fire they fuse to the architecture—
        their spirits the exhaust rushing now
            through our vowels, only in a different way.
            Like the spirits rising up
                from cracked beers.
                Their posthumous jeremiads
                bidding us: *Listen.*
                    As hawks curve over the
                    horizon like reason
                    in the ugly argument: *Party.*
                    Like he who knows
                    the answer is sometimes
                    flame. He who paints
                    the exit maps of the heart,
                    knowing

                    we won't ever
                    read them.

MUSICALLY SPEAKING

I go in, head back as if swallowing a bell.
A note in my diaphragm
of more frankness than sound.
Is that the story?
The voice within flexing its horn,
the one note
not to hit
rising from the face?
I try to think of something you once sang.
Quickly I make jazz hands.
But the tone
we are left with
sinks
into the cracks you see
along the otherwise
perfect floor

PRE ELEGY FOR AN ABSOLUTE SUPERIOR

A truth broke from the air
or the current of a borrowed book
in which Spanish
soldiers feed orphaned boys
slivers of avocado. Here
there is so much with permission to fall
all day on narrow streets
there but not there. Not yet
a tremendous chord.

The wind shakes a stop sign
and I stop. It is here
I put my own hand
on my shoulder and pretend,
in a silent film,
to articulate a motion
that wont backfire.
This is before you leave.
Before you leave,
on the edge of here
there is a famous tree
which holds your increase.
It has no plans to let go.

CRYPTOBIOSIS

Staying up with the seamonkeys past one a.m.,
books wave their pages. *World Book*
encyclopedias from the year of your birth,
rubbing their spines after long-drawn-out sleep.

In the flapping pages, you begin to see
not your childhood, your early luster,
but the tiny connectors and miniature feelers
doing the work of the fever. Their lines
refer the reader back to sketches by Kurt

Vonnegut appearing in the preface to the story
of the little sea: carefully packed, tiny
bodies drop in bundles on the sea floor,
are undone the way utterance undoes silence.

AUSTRALOPITHECUS INTERRUPTUS

Five ex-courtesans lie around a hot spring.
The coldest temperature bests a low set
three point eight million years ago. The rest
is not so simple: the cauliflowered ear
grizzled with merit, the almost sexless dream:
My being bashed by waves, against white rocks,
whereby I leave the clear indentation
of soft membranes. The ex-courtesans, hands full
of gold figurines, spout water and sing
a cappella songs about the layering of anticipation.
They spark a hissing fire, toast the nightfall's
hairy dark. Me, I feather my casual pockets,
go back to New Jersey. For so long, wait for discovery
of the few brittle tools known to be buried,
which have not been found this whole year
of concentration—a year nearly sexless if
you don't count beating on my own cave.
Times, reaching up, I released what was caught.

OCTOPUS

In the theater of the divided,
I octopus—

like a contorted human
form. I go

back to the sunken deck,
retrieve what sank:

In the hull,
the few vowels.

I'm wanting
to recover the legs of you

wrap them over my arms
like devices new

swimmers use
to ignore drowning.

It's this going that's the *Jesus*.
Just thinking about it
a nervous shirt.

I do not sleep:
Volumes my hand retracts
dominating

certain pillows or fogs.
Reading the manuals
of muscles

built in mid-air
until way past curfew.
Once (worse) upon a time:

A tight-rope-walker, mid-wire,
tuning his hands
to the awkward weight

of his gloves. Reaching
like an erector set
into the mist

where it is possible
our wounds are symbolic
and we are only

wanting in growth.
I have learned
a body will form

shoots, multiplicities even
to be read.
Lifting into the rain

or out of city cabs,
I draw mine into me.
It is trying to buy the world

a Coke. One hand is
galloping
down my body.

The whole distance assumes
a darned shadow.

Part Two

EAST

The hurricane digs for its salt white dress
the wilds of which are filled with want   Using its pistons

Forms a crude 9   Our place

Is like empty drams for it   The hurricane dreams
of logarithms   It is beautiful

The miles in profile swing   stroked over dress

One form   most blessed in aft—
no, *Eye*, because the world is boring.

SOUTH

A compost heap's genius is you have seen a meditation

if you have looked upon rinds,
the clippings of your own eyes
the warp of paisley   leaf gassing down like peels.

But you who are
no longer here (hello out there)

your open mile dips

so gracefully   where it would merge
with empty clothes lines   on a Sunday   nice day
and then another.

YOU'LL NEVER GET TO SLEEP NOW

Girl's eyes, opera, flax, container, dew.
We were trying to spellbind time.

Do you, Sora, at dusk,
remember
boiling the everyday names of things?

Getting off
on hostile smells?

What we started to say.

Hair fire.
Honeysuckle bloom.

To worm the tongue
away from each word.

Not sleeping?

Two for no sleep.
Two in bed, projecting

wall-shadows of a prior bird
now flown—

two finding
(hands full of dark)

the more it takes shape,
the more it loses out to light.

ALTAR BOYS OF THE SACRED HEART

As we live, so shall we duck
out of sight, crawl
on all fours near the footnotes.

I'm getting better
like after
the Feast of San Gennaro,

but if I have
a darkness, a certain
'80's kind

of sadness,
it's from whole hours
spent cloistered

undefined in dark robes. Long after
shadows will
have crept the altar

and backed themselves away.
After Lent has come
and is gone.

This time, what will you give up?
I would
have answered

those ashes
of the burning palm.

HOMESICKNESS

A lake with your first name.
Along a hollowed-out hill.

You'll take it as a sign.
Into the anatomy of bells.

Walk it into a ring of stones.
Drag it through a South

Jersey town whose stark marquees
predict the neutral-sounding

eternity. All "what-ifs" suffer
as technology lags. For instance

the mouth has a weather—
no one notices the red

phone inside it. Colors and things halved
we want to have sex with.

Children see an obelisk
flowering into the stars. The children

bouncing on a bundle of moss.
Tense until the day they can smoke

out night windows with a view
of the last great campfire

redolent with the burning of letters.
Until the day we say anything will do.

Kisses and information.
Try lipstick and the lake will confess.

Like an August with laws.

Uphill. February. It had to be something small because a day was all you had.

Vestibule. Psyche. Memory.

One place and then the next.

TWELVE BAR BLUES

What are unresolved are the blunt, frenetic gusts,
the launching of ill-intoned oratorios
over the tips of high hedges. A serenade
so harsh I might be moved to ship
a severed ear to its final notes. Tonight, I will ride
a two-seated cycle over those
modest hills. You'll find them just below
the day's end's cloud vamping
like *Muddy and The Wolf;* its big toe
thumping bass. How I think of Martha's feelings—
behind their latticework, shaken
from the interstate's vibrato. Like them,
I miss the tulips of each evening
pounding death. "Can we talk about this?"
they seem to say over and over. The banner of stray words
behind each one: *Want you / into / my life.*

MOTHERGIG

Today, one of us carried her
over the courtyard, small instruments
wound into her hair.

Outside, a summer evening.
We restore blown-over ornaments.

We gather them like gathering in
a continuous breath
against the house and the neighbors',

tracing them entirely
until I know I am home.
Yet the wind is only absent.

As if the clapping back door,
the echoing shutters,
have all run down their batteries.

As a child, I loved
only their lilting. Now, they lack
any real rhythmic point.

Or the wind won't lift the weight of things.
Or is curtailing any music
inside this territory.

EXACTA

That time I bet on *Tender Mist* to win, I also bet on *Flaming Heart* to show.
Leaving the racetrack, I wasn't surprised to find a boy stealing
the caution light from one of those shock-orange drums
that ease us back into a lane. The expressway
heaving out like a cloud. On the bend
of exit 16, cars just missing him
like the backs of hands, like the final words
of a blown joke.

As I slept, houses strung together like one Connecticut.
Late-night, the sky a vast headboard
east of here. Across the country,
in everyone's dream:

A few inky colts.
A sunset cloud vista.
A commercial for antidepressants
urging the ill to come forward.

THERE THERE, BALTIMORE

Where climate ends the local gaze is unrestrained and free
of expansionist gradations.

A jetliner eight miles out glides in like a blown kiss.
A distant, cultish spasm its record of process.

Like one who stands in a gravel road, thrusts out his
unloved
parts then bends them down.

First an alarm would take hold:
a dark bird's trill. A prison jumpsuit's engine-rev.

The very nightfall is a series of like correspondences,
longitudes and yardsticks designed

to measure the disparate parts of the self.
The need to be handed back whole comes from banishment

to be reflected on later. This very nightfall
a rubber ball keeps vigil. What is the satellite thinking?

There are no instructions upon landing.
One must open one's eyes for there is a city.

The pilot makes contact with the ground,
and the Holy Spirit for whom wind is the ex-rear-engine.

I BORDERING YOU

The ease with which you come
from that direction.
If it isn't the slipping past

it's the washing over.
Like a saying. You are becoming
a tunneller. The wire is

tearing your slacks as if
you are restricted to a loop
of trails on the edge

of a bean field. Zone
where other survivors cower
and brainstorm.

Two summers in
between exploratory fringe
and the orange

light of billboards. You do
not say a thing
about arriving whole.

EMPURPLED

"To carry any lie to fruition, it must open

to the horizon or close forever."

His thresholds you cannot see.

Once detected, aren't we more alive in the white heat?

Telling anyone who will listen, "It's my job,

filling in the shape of this absence."

The touch of a hand, maybe. A breast.

Two oranges in a tight-fitting shirt.

Imagine a piebald lie: "I'm Artie. I'm nice."

When really, before dark, I'm smothering the specimens

from behind. All those rhythmic

feelings being seized. *Downtown*, where

I used to think the wind moved

because we had it surrounded. And now I think

there is no end to those I wouldn't touch.

SON OF A JUMPER

Belief we are in ditch. Its vague ebb parted only by a path.
Blackberries. A little medicine.

Having forgotten to graph the clean line
of matters one couldn't string

never mind amnesia for what
has traced the exterior trying to sustain its myth.

Today, the power lines have jumped inside the trees.
Lenses, like alibis have changed:

Take the forgotten name for a starving herd.
Snow into rain back into snow.

On which couch do we commit this
hour of our history, the surface

willing like earthenware in our minds?
Many boys were laughed right

out of the ditch. Red, having flunked middle-air.
Fliers beaten by the same sky

lurk behind their eyes, to wrap in the ether
what held before the failure.

VISCERA

On the way to get ICE, again, we fall for this district: Sudden rhythms out long windows, to an eye: scoops of field. A bus stop. The blur of suburban barns. But the heart of hearts is a 70's porno mag lying behind the orphanage. With it comes a thin vinyl recording of a hate-fuck. It is spring. Because of science. We wind the clocks. Because the radio is full of static, the laws that govern our listening are written, nearby, on the thick roadside air. In the weeds. To us as kids. The way the sum writes back to the total of its parts.

TRY LOVING SOMEONE WHO DOESN'T LOVE YOU

Try approaching the light so sloshed all you do
is rise in the wafting breeze,

                                        tuck your two

immense wings in,
click your thorax and go
outside.

In a stuttered sort of flight,
little circles,
before falling in love.

                                        Wings the color of bark?

                    Sure.
                    All the emotion

                                powdery

                                        unnamable

and worse:
Brightness is
what she's made of.

                                        As a result

the earth
never contradicts the sun.

In a fractured everafter,

                                        outcomes such as August, July.

BETWEEN THE LIONS

Inside my strategy, the mice
of my becoming
collapse on their wheels.

You are upset
by the mice, their not being
great beasts.

My fight or flight response,
you say, is more like sweat or smoke—

Who knows what I would do
if challenged by rhinos
in the place we rent.

And it's the same
in my recurring dream:

You strap your hands to the receptors
of my all-night zone.

Army-crawling
through the vent shafts,
I carry you, safely,

to a loft with high ceilings.
To the definite world

where I would be a lover
scurrying up your dress
with the treed raccoon.

THE END OF WINTER

Buildings don't coalesce spelling I-I-I,
holding still all day. Like a bridge above water:

Steam shrouds the bridge as it does
a hotdog vendor's many code violations.

Says the cabbie, "I soothsay and soothsay,"
trying to out-flank the parade.

Bag-women can-can through a revolving door.
In the iron district, ladies-of-waiting find

few men to circumscribe. The bright
snaps on their purses yawn and rust open.

Who says we sing *Help* before singing
Come Together? On a street of old letters,

of storm-tossed buildings. "It's the only place
I can go for relief." But as we wander in

through the breath, we find a view
enjoyed only via Xerox, and know this

only compounds space, in the overlong equation
of air over city. In the skylight, for example,

pages of clouds out just for a walk.
From a window, a boy of uncertain age disappears

behind an unfinished schoolhouse—
ten pages of his being struck by celebratory

gunfire. Waving, he signals: *Ok, Ok*.

NOTES ON THE DANCE

In, lovemaking is the freeway sound
coming through the trees. Who could sleep?
Piano hammers roll every noise, again.
The roads, out, are blocked. Then not.
There you are, under a loadbearing wall,
a body crashed on the couch, and in
shaky sunlight. As it warms you, a residue
with the sheeniest of sheens pools up
in your eye. A screen door slams from
being open all day like your eyes that are
the color of TV. You have your father to thank
for that. Thank mother they are full
of chemicals which agitate themselves, molecules
that cannot stop spinning. When you wake,
alone, slowly pulling off pieces of tuxedo,
dismissing love like an old puppeteer
gently relieving his marionette of its limbs:
When the corsage on its chest snaps a picture
of his neck, it swoons like a kite-like flower.

COGNITIVE BEHAVIORIAL

Then one counselor seated
along the dirty wall

whispers: "Next time you step
out of the shower, try

first drying your foot."
Or, if first toweling the fore-

arms is your thing, try
first drying a leg." A long

silence follows (I leave
the room for a cream soda,

come back feeling almost
nothing). "I wonder if

you'd try this," the nurse says.
"Instead of going straight

for your genitalia, try first
drying your back. This

is quite consistent with
the type of change required."

AT THE SEMI-ANNUAL ANIMA RETREAT
I GO LOOKING FOR MY FEMALE SIDE

For one dollar a guy dreaming of an eagle soaring
up the sky then turning to eat its own wings.
Holding him two beefy men in lamplight.
This, other reenactments, all behind the velvet rope.
If anything, what begins when we exhale
our names? This year's guests wear bathing suits,
their bodies working swiftly at existence.
On this day of all days, upright for the hunt;
How long would it lie there, unknown, customary?
I sit between two interior perspectives
until lightning hits, until a symbol of the soul
washes ashore, is de-bearded, rises into the sky.
The wind blowing us senseless. My guide says sooner
or later, rain. Says my teary eyes will suddenly
come. Says, "Walk toward the violin to make it play."

LYRIC

Arrival is much larger than my body.
Deep waves adjust on the edge of the sea.
Farther east, the bright registers.

The actuality of hunger
is its cause. I hear the sound
of waves breaking in a small space

like false speech fetching
after its own words.

We aren't the eyes that blink when lying.
Two repeating eyes—
when half-lovers carry a second map or a habit

all the tracks of departure
are made underwater.

It is here we store May along the soft
rigging of our breath.

The roads are always open
they are the equivalent of old texts
which drain their dark words onto our knees.

ANOTHER LIFE

I find myself believing in your complete refurbishment.

Last night it was, as *world* was remodeled,
                                        your core
blasting out to the ends of blue.
Reaching for the newest tools, I opened little prayers.

Someone cited, "crudity and brushstrokes"
on the canvas of your religion—

But I thought of that Caravaggio, where a painted-over Apostle
        still lurks.

A ghost image, yes, but the light from Christ's plate
reflects back on his face.

Nowhere in a still-life is light like that.

Grab up your fruit, your heavy shoe.
Inside your own half-darkness, try tiptoeing toward the open arms.

Part Three

Terrible Imitation, here is
the third bed where you lay

the august thing down.
Here is the stepladder

to the sublime. Here is
the book of sad lithographs

we will press you into
don't cry. Here is the Dark-

Eyed-Junco you prefer,
famous for grappling

long nights. When you
wake, when you sit,

and your final painting
is there. As many

paintings as you like. Here,
here are the literal

interior fields, here are
the muddy boots.

CRAYOLA PASTORAL

Fall's fat crayon
drawn from its holster
like a delayed thesis.
It gets tangled
in a tree near the border.
And yet understanding
bounds homeward,
even if under-
standing is out of work
like any number
of Dada objects
adorning a restaurant wall.
We are blessed.
No longer must
our foreigners teach us
the colors of warfare
when it pours down at night
and no women
are left on the porch:
To get acquainted
with the lines
we abstracted inhabit.
To burrow,
the first half of morning,
into myth.
To live on the hills,
to draw them, their essence.
To color in
the book of animals
receiving Fall,
not the book of Fall
receiving animals.

OCTOBER

A team of new citizens forms a circle widening.
Our new citizens— the landscape crew

for an old movie star. Fanning out
in the gold mountain grass and back,

they trail garlands of lady's dying vine
to a barrel. Their movements flush a few terns

up the afternoon. Minus the country
in relief, all the trees turn to stilts.

Immediately, the crew sees straight up
sky, and a figure of their host confirmed

only by the outline of her thighs.
It's the old actress. Emerging from the rooms

of her house. Standing at the patio's edge,
she holds up her skirt filled with birds.

DURING A LONG SPELL OF FLOOD

More like the laws of a leaning world,
what that means across miles.
If our empties are not our empties.
Nor the contour of water itself to the eye.
How its rising will chase us upstairs
to rehearse the rasp of risen ghosts
coming unstuck. There is little sense of the way it once was:
the courtyard in the shape of a star.

Two birds sing: *who's so beat, we're so beat.*
We see them trying to meet with the sky
and boomeranging back. A dark permanent distance.
The room, the new backwater, languorous.

As the leaning world leans we write hymns to survival.
When three priests arrive
they must climb on our blue Volvo to reach us.
We remove our shoes.
My wife says, "Hey, you vessels, don't touch
me if you are going to touch
that wire. Don't look at us as if
the graying heads of dandelions
aren't drifting through the hold of our house."

MADONNA AND CHILD WITH HELICOPTER
~15th century, French

Sleet dismounts off the slate roof onto what God has made.
We also think God is the sleet
lasting not long before he must go become the light
playing with a grandmother's hair—
all a composed hologram with her whirring in the center
if only for an instant.
What is the center but an imperfect muscle
spasmodically flexing?
Beyond the border a string a blade an ending.
Credits roll like busses through a more fragrant world,
carrying, as they ascend each hill,
a conspicuous lack of names.
For a brief time what flew flew convincingly.
The sky was tethered to a tree nearby,
escorting the sun in a loose shell,
a boy's face having been there before.
Where is everyone today?
To say nothing of the empty ladder
stiff in the unlit stairwell.
Or the elevator slow to return
empty from the upper floors.
November when it is
our Hoboken, and we go to the window
find a machine already hovering there.
Or a nightingale. Or the rammer
of heads into paradise.

SOMETIMES FINCH

I was the finch in your poem
when you were the you
of your attic.

Perennially, some things were a watercolor.

The windows clouded
from the blue
exhaust all day
curling into the alley.

The walls
turning black from the candles
the way *heart*

grows somber
when you have to move a piano
into the wind.

No explanation skylight
to reveal the mutability

of fireflies lifting
over your head,
or to remind you

I've been alone.

When what begins as bird,
transfigured—
a one-ounce fist landing on the keys.

AS THE YARD DARKENS

My first impulse, after you pile junk around me
(pans, crankshafts, used defibrillators)
is to let every piece fill with rain
until, weighed down, all spring into the shapes
of dumb memorabilia,
like your suit of armor made from muscle-car parts
to really show the bees.
I watch the leveling out of batted water.
My hallucinations
like partitions.

As the yard darkens, your canaries loop, molt, and go bald.
Your rabbits nose a mostly empty can.
Your garden grows only a hybrid forgiveness.
When I see your face
in some moonlit metal, it's mouthing:
All / this / rolled / out / time,
until we both confess
with the heft and resolve of two engines.
From the weight of rain
and the unconscious patina on the tin—
right there inside a rusting drum a used pump labors.

ROOSTER FROM THE ROMANTICS

This one who books it after only the slightest of stimuli
treads a grid of yeses in the mud.
Remember others in the trap
did not get a stay. That one in Jerusalem or that one
in the backyard immobile in a foul hole.
I was reading the wall and the quiet, suburbanites,
when I saw him
up and walking his chalk circle,
too nonplussed to crow.
Various possibilities will end us at dusk.
In other words, now, morning
will embellish all its major announcements:
And just like that a nasty kite
swung into the street.
Rain gurgling in the gutters
spilled in a powerful overflow
nearer to God.

THE PAINTER'S WIFE

My faculties buck
at what you say is bleak,
when it's only the half-
light on the lawn;
when the Easy Mart
has shut off its sign.
You say, to create tension,
I should stand
in one-third of your life,
sunsets painted
on my sunglasses.
But I'm over believing
your hypothesis
of how black, inside a bruise,
will lean against blue.
You say, *the opposite of love
is indifference—*
hate being only
for effect. But I've seen
your portraits of
embraceable madams,
your book-length collection
of headboard slats—
empty themes
I look forward to leaving.
Here, where the wind
keeps on dividing,
my mission is
to reunite you with truth—
Between you,
seas rage.
Above you, the wind
interrogates.

LAME DUCK POPE

Our lady of headless statue, pray for us.

Our lady of one shaky wing.

Our lady of runaway stumbling barefoot,

by the river where we live.

O lady of a Carl Jung *shadow,*

O limb fallen from the oak.

Our lady is Mother Superior.

Our home is the screened in porch.

O lady of burning bakery fat

by the river where we live.

O lay-folk lapsing into pope-a-dope.

Hey Cleveland, we are live.

O rector of forms rigid by heart.

O this, and how edicts drain you.

Those regret geese are back, and twenty four
hours later they have traveled deeper than ever
into our bustling city, as water travels deeper inside
a wind-up watch: stopping the hands, stranding
the numeric date. So as we walk into the chapel all
God talks about is a time before this one, in which
totally false confessions flew from an old canvas
bag. Not a flame inside your holiness. The tragedy
of water is all around us like a bottled up message
inching its way around the Cape of Good Hope.
We've been talking up the movie version where
Bill Paxton plays the stranded. It would ask: how
do you locate someone who everyday wakes
before his solar calculator can call him a zero, is
out the door before his God can break it off with
him like Madagascar, floating into the sunset?

COCCYX

Coordinates ran miles made
entirely of quiet. Lower and no devil knew.
     Leaden everyone. Horizontal
    while the elements were hemmed by
        a blushing new light
    that punctures through each keyhole
        to the room's true center.
  It is said an arc runs from
  foot to heart. Ring to heart.
        We look down shoes. Regard our thighs
          against the backdoor flap, our legs
       in the air. To be geometric
   like a sail. To arc like a pear being
      seized by a honky-tonk king.
   What is divisible like us?
   A drill of large jays
   windblown to plumb?
   Spine
   thy god staggered seeds down
   like houses
   in a magazine. Will you stay with me?
   Through the maze of the hour,
   the touching of
   each keyhole.
   I'll be ready when you come.

GIRLIGIG

It begins with watching:
Three wind-blades (spinning
for amusement) move
two dancer's hips. Every-
thing mechanical as existence.
The body's logic
continues behind the subdivision
to summon truth: morning
lifts its cute blue skirt,
a sunflower bends to meet it.
Each time, a different version of the dance
I didn't think about.
Gradually, content from a dream
sinks in: a small crew
tearing down a wooden church
no one has paid any homage in.
Happening upon
an endless mirror, the men
are reproduced in miniature:
the steeple in their hands,
small as the fingerbone of a saint.

MEMORIAL ACCLAMATION

When the neighbor dressed as High Priest
decides to invoke the vatic, wind-ripples appear
    on my Kool-ade. "The Lamb of God," he says,
     "*His* final costume for this world." He encourages us
         to gather more candy, but we drag our
          billowing pillowcases, or even ignore them like
      amorphous clouds in the last frame of sky
        about to be absorbed into a larger, darker system.
       In the curve of adolescence, eventually, all
       routine suffers. Costumes such as a slightly-
           stylized-child-pirate, once popular, are altogether
     phased out. In rewind, the melted candy re-
         forms around the safety pin, and the story
of awareness starts again. Truly, in shifting
the patch to my other eye, I have taught
myself to do nothing. My words, eventually,
     parroted.
        At night, as the High Priest
        smudges us with
        smoke from a burning urn,
        he says:
        "Leave your radios on
        until dawn.
        By morning, you will hear, honking
        on the Soul album of
        your resolve,
        golden saxophones
        laziness/ has/ risen/ from."

NOT DYING

Gazing. Nothing's happened to the breath,
epitomized by the ocean wave of the moment.
It doesn't take for you to see, eventually,
blue herons the size of handbags on the horizon.
Once I saw two hummingbirds with
copper-colored chests
mating where the bungalow porch
curves like something foreign in the summer.
Yes swooping from the beams
to the complaints in the trees.
We do not know what will happen.
We know what will happen. It is easier
than it has ever been.
Someone tells you go stand there
among the lanterns, now
that the sky is clear and we are all in the picture.
I've never seen mandrakes that large ever.
They remind me: what is underneath is anything
but. There is another axis under that.
And a hung white sheet.
A gust of wind will fill the open mouths with air:
And what someone may owe us,
when we do die, flies by like a bullet.

NOTES

Pg. 4
"Burying A St. Joseph In The Backyard" comes from the Italian American tradition of burying a St. Joseph statue in the yard in order to aid in the quick sale of a house.

Pg. 7
Axis Bold As Love is a Jimi Hendrix album.

Pg. 8
"Smoke On the Water" is a Deep Purple song.

Pg. 15
"Cryptobiosis" is a reversible state in which an animal's metabolism has come to a virtual standstill…such as with the sea monkey.

Pg. 24
The Feast of San Gennaro is the annual feast that brings over one million people to the streets of Little Italy, NYC in the annual salute to the patron saint of Naples.

Pg. 32
"…it must open to the horizon or close forever" refers loosely to a statement by Donald Hall referring to how a poet should think about constructing the final lines of a poem.

Pg. 37
"Help" and "Come Together" are Beatles songs.

Pg. 41
Muddy and the Wolf is a collaborative album by Muddy Waters and Howlin' Wolf.

Pg. 42
"Another Life" is for Russell Dillon.

Pg. 59
"Changing Back" is for Matt Salerno.

Pg. 62
"Not Dying" is for Irene Soliwoda.

CHRISTOPHER SALERNO was born and raised in New Jersey and currently lives in Raleigh, NC. His poems have appeared or are forthcoming in journals such as: Colorado Review, Jubilat, Electronic Poetry Review, AGNI-online, Spinning Jenny, Forklift Ohio, LIT, GoodFoot, Barrow Street, River City, Carolina Quarterly, and in the anthology, "The Bedside Guide To No Tell Motel." He currently teaches in the English Department at North Carolina State University.

SPUYTEN DUYVIL

All Spuyten Duyvil titles are available through your local bookseller via
Booksense.com

Distributed to the trade by
Biblio Distribution
a division of NBN
1-800-462-6420
http://bibliodistribution.com

All Spuyten Duyvil authors may be contacted at
authors@spuytenduyvil.net

Author appearance information and background at
http://spuytenduyvil.net